The Dynar

Vinegar and Baking Soda

A Two-Volume Set Containing:

Vinegar Solutions: Money Saving, Green Ideas for Cleaning, Cooking and Health

and

Baking Soda Solutions: Economical, Eco-Friendly Ideas for Your House, Your Yard and You

M.B. Ryther

Copyright © 2012 M.B. Ryther

All rights reserved.

ISBN-13: 978-1481055413

ISBN-10: 1481055410

To John, David, Nick, Emily and Lucy.

For all your love and patience.

TABLE OF CONTENTS

Book One: Vinegar Solutions

Vinegar, Who Knew?	1
Kitchen Hints	4
Laundry Helps	8
Bathroom Solutions	11
All Around the House	13
Outside Ideas	18
Kids and Pets	22
Cooking Tips	24
Health and Hygiene	27
Blood Sugar and Weight Loss	31
Acknowledgements	35

Book Two: Baking Soda Solutions

Baking Soda 101	37
Kitchen Aid	43
Cooking Tips	51
Laundry Solutions	54
Bathroom Benefits	57
Nursery Help	60
All Around the House	63
Pets and Pests	68
Garage and Shop	71
Yard and Garden	74
Sports and Recreation	77
Crafts and Play	80
Health and Hygiene	83
Bibliography	89
About the Author	91

Vinegar Solutions

Money Saving, Green Ideas for Cleaning, Cooking and Health

By M.B. Ryther

Copyright © 2012 M.B. Ryther
All rights reserved.

VINEGAR, WHO KNEW?

The Multi-Purpose Product

Most of us know that vinegar will clean a coffeemaker and shine a window. And, of course, everyone knows that it's great on salads. But did you know that it can also clean your jewelry, kill your weeds, keep fleas off your dog, and deodorize a room? And you may not know this either: Scientific studies conducted within the last decade show vinegar to be effective in helping people with type 2 diabetes control their blood glucose levels.

The truth is, vinegar can do all that and more. In fact, vinegar can do so much around the house that there may be little need for that stash of cleaning products under the sink. Unlike many of those products, vinegar is non-abrasive, so it's safe to use on even the most delicate glassware. It's also non-toxic, allowing it to be used harmlessly around kids and pets. Without a doubt, there are few products available today that are as versatile as vinegar, as effective, as safe, and as cheap.

Vinegar Basics

Vinegar (from the French word vinaigre, "sour wine") is mostly water containing an active ingredient of acetic acid. It is made from a variety of raw materials such as fruits, grains, sugars, syrups, and wine, which are fermented to form ethyl alcohol. To this is added acetic acid-forming bacteria which converts the alcohol to vinegar. The many varieties of vinegar (distilled white, apple cider, wine, malt, and garlic, among others) are determined by the raw materials used, as well as by the fermenting and distilling processes.

Vinegar History

Vinegar has been around for a long time. The ancient Babylonians were the first to turn wine into vinegar, sometime around 5,000 B.C. The idea of "soured wine" eventually passed down to the Greeks and Romans, whose literature abounds with passages reflecting its popularity. Hippocrates, for example, used vinegar as an antibiotic. Helen of Troy bathed in it as a way of relaxing. And Cleopatra supposedly dissolved her pearls in vinegar to win a bet with Mark Antony that she could consume a fortune in a single meal.

By 1,000 B.C. many Oriental cultures had discovered the food preserving quality of vinegar and added spices to improve its taste. During the Black Plague of the Middle Ages, thieves poured vinegar over their hands before robbing the dead to ward off germs. And during the seventeenth century, Europeans commonly used vinegar as a deodorant and deodorizer; the aristocracy would often be seen holding vinegar-scented sponges to their noses to mask the smell of offensive street sewage. In American history, vinegar was reportedly used during the Civil War to treat and prevent scurvy, and later used in World War I to treat wounds of soldiers.

A Few Recommendations

- Unless stated otherwise, simple distilled white vinegar of the least expensive variety will work just fine for most of the ideas in this book. Save the more expensive gourmet vinegars for your palette.

- Get a couple of spray bottles to keep solutions of vinegar and water–or straight undiluted vinegar–handy in your kitchen, your laundry room, your garage, or wherever you keep your cleaning supplies.

- Don't assume that mixing vinegar with one of your other cleansers will enhance that product's effectiveness. It could be dangerous. The acetic acid in vinegar when mixed with some lavatory bowl cleaners, for example, produces a deadly chlorine gas.

- Don't get too hung up on exact measurements, even though you will see suggested ratios in many of the tips printed here. They are just that, *suggestions*. Even different vinegar makers and other published household tipsters will sometimes differ on whether to use a 1/2 cup vs. whole cup, etc. Use the given suggestions as a guideline at first, and adjust when and if you feel it's necessary. Don't be afraid of using your instinct. A "splash" in many cases is just as good as a measured tablespoon.

Now, go into the kitchen and grab that bottle–the vinegar bottle, that is!

KITCHEN HINTS

Clean the coffeemaker

Fill the pot with water and a cup of vinegar. Run through the normal cycle and let stand until it cools. Then rinse with a cycle of plain water.

Deodorize the kitchen drain

Pour a cup of vinegar down the drain once a week. Let it stand for 30 minutes and then flush with cold water.

Clean and deodorize the garbage disposal

Make ice cubes out of a cup of vinegar and enough water to fill the ice tray. Then feed the cubes down the disposal. After grinding, run cold water through for about a minute.

Eliminate onion odor from hands

Rub vinegar on your fingers before and after slicing onions to cut the smell.

Remove fruit stains from your hands

Simply rub them in vinegar.

Disinfect fresh produce

Fill your sink with a gallon of cold water and add 4 tablespoons of white or apple cider vinegar. Rinse your fruits and vegetables in this solution to get rid of dirt, germs, pesticides, and insects.

Clean the drainboard

Get rid of hard water stains by pouring vinegar over the board (or soaking it in the sink if easier) and letting it set overnight. Rub the stains off in the morning.

Clean and disinfect cutting boards

Wipe with full-strength vinegar.

Clean the microwave

Boil a solution of 1/4 cup vinegar and 1 cup of water in the microwave. Will loosen splattered-on food and deodorize.

Get stains and odors out of pots

Fill pot with a solution of vinegar and water. Boil until stains loosen and can be washed away.

Unclog a drain

Pour a handful of baking soda down the drain and add a 1/2 cup of vinegar. Then rinse with cold water.

Freshen a lunchbox

Soak a piece of bread in vinegar and let it set in the lunchbox overnight.

Clean a thermos

Fill with 1/4 cup of vinegar and warm water. Add some uncooked rice to help rub off grime. Put the lid on and shake vigorously. Rinse out and allow to air dry.

Clean the refrigerator

Use a solution of equal parts vinegar and water to wash out grime and food odors.

Clean and deodorize jars

Eliminate odors from those mayonnaise, peanut butter, and mustard jars you save by rinsing them with vinegar when empty.

Clean a teapot

Boil a mixture of water and vinegar in the teapot. Then wipe away the dirt and grime easily.

Get rid of dishwasher spots

Add a 1/2 cup of vinegar to the second rinse.

Clean the dishwasher

Place a cup of vinegar on the bottom rack, and then, with no other dishes in the washer, run a complete cycle. Do this once a month to reduce soap buildup on the inner mechanisms.

Make drinking glasses sparkle

Add a cup of vinegar to a sink of warm, soapy water and wash glasses by hand to remove cloudiness and spots. (Works well with china and fine glassware too.)

Clean stainless steel and chrome

Remove spots from stainless steel by wiping with a vinegar-dampened cloth.

Cut grease and odors on dishes

Add a splash or more of vinegar to hot, soapy wash water.

Remove coffee and tea stains from china

Use equal parts vinegar and salt to loosen and remove stains from china cups.

Remove tarnish from copper pots and utensils

Brush a thin coating of vinegar over the tarnish and apply an even coating of salt. Then rub away the tarnish with a dry cloth and rinse in hot water.

Clean faucets and taps

To remove tough mineral deposits on faucets, wrap them in cloths or paper towels soaked in vinegar. Cover the area in plastic wrap to prevent evaporation. Wait an hour or two, and then wash away the sediment with a soft brush or cloth. Rinse and dry.

Get rid of cooking smells

Let simmer on the stovetop a small pot of equal parts vinegar and water.

LAUNDRY HELPS

Unclog the steam iron

Pour equal amounts of vinegar and water into the iron's water chamber. Turn to "steam" and leave the iron on for five minutes in an upright position. Then unplug and allow to cool. Any loose particles should come out when you empty the water.

Clean a scorched iron plate

Make a paste of salt and heated vinegar. Rub onto the surface of a cool iron to remove dark or burned-on stains.

Remove starch on an iron

Wipe the plate of a cold iron with vinegar.

Iron out dryer wrinkles

Get rid of wrinkles caused by a too-hot or too-long dryer cycle by ironing over the wrinkles with a "pressing cloth" dampened with vinegar. (Works for hemline creases too.)

Maintain your washer

Once a month, pour a cup of vinegar into the washer (without any added clothes) and run it through a normal cycle to remove unwanted soap residue.

Brighten and soften fabrics

Add up to one cup of vinegar to the rinse cycle to break up soap buildup, thereby brightening and softening the fabrics.

Put fluff in the blankets

Add two cups of vinegar in the rinse cycle for loads of cotton and wool blankets.

Keep clothes static-and-lint free

Yep, you guessed it. Add a cup of vinegar to the rinse cycle.

Keep colors from running

Immerse clothes in full-strength vinegar before washing.

Fix a shrunken sweater

Boil a shrunken wool garment in one part vinegar and two parts water for 25 minutes. Reshape the garment and allow to air dry.

Whiten socks

For the most bleach-resistant, grime-laden socks, try this: In a large pot, add a cup of vinegar to 1 1/2 quarts of water and bring to a boil. Then pour the piping hot solution into a bucket, toss in the dingy sock, and let them soak overnight. The next day, wash as usual.

Take grease off of suede

Dip a toothbrush in vinegar and gently brush over the grease spot. Allow to dry.

Remove tough stains

Rub vinegar gently over wine, cola, fruit, jam, mustard, coffee, deodorant, and perspiration stains. Then wash as usual.

Get the smoke smell out of clothes (without washing)

Add a cup of vinegar to a bathtub of hot water. Hang clothes above the steam.

Soften drapes

Add a few drops of vinegar to the rinse cycle when laundering drapes or synthetic curtains to soften and reduce static.

Pamper your nylons

Add a splash of vinegar to two quarts of wash water to make nylons gleam and last longer.

Remove salt and water stains from boots and shoes

Wipe with full-strength vinegar to remove salt and water stains. Polish if desired.

Clean black patent leather shoes

Wipe with a solution of vinegar and water to remove spots.

Prevent clothesline freeze

Wipe clothesline with a vinegar-dampened cloth to prevent clothes from sticking to the line in cold weather.

BATHROOM SOLUTIONS

Clean plastic shower curtains

Wash in the machine along with a bath towel. Then add a cup of vinegar to the rinse cycle. Will make the curtains soft and pliable, as well as remove soap and grime buildup.

Clean a removable shower head

Soak in a container of vinegar overnight. Will unclog holes due to mineral deposits and remove corrosion.

Clean a fixed shower head (or faucet)

Wrap a vinegar-saturated cloth around the shower head or faucet and leave on overnight. Wipe away the grime the next day. Alternatively, fill a plastic bag with undiluted vinegar and attach it around the shower head with a rubber band or tape. Leave it overnight or check it after a few hours to see if it makes a difference.

Shine your fixtures

Dampen a sponge or cloth with full-strength vinegar and wipe down chrome, stainless steel, ceramic, or plastic fixtures. Polish with a soft cloth.

Clean the toilet bowl

Use full-strength vinegar and a sturdy brush to remove stubborn stains. Deodorize the bowl by pouring in 3 cups of vinegar and letting it sit for 30-60 minutes before flushing.

Clean tile grout

Use full-strength vinegar and a brush to clean grout and remove mildew.

Clean tub and tile surfaces

Wipe away rings and soap film with full-strength vinegar. Rinse with water. For tough tub rings, fill the tub with hot water (enough to cover the rings) and mix in three cups of full-strength vinegar. Let it sit for four hours. The ring should wipe away fairly easily after that.

Clean and polish glass shower doors

Wipe with a vinegar and water solution to make doors sparkle.

Unstiffen a toothbrush

Soak in hot vinegar for 30 minutes and rinse out.

Clean combs and hairbrushes

First, remove as much loose hair as possible from the combs and brushes. Then combine 2 teaspoons of shampoo and 1/4 cup of white vinegar in a clean sink or bucket filled with warm/hot water. Submerge the combs and brushes in the solution allow to soak for 10 to 15 minutes. Afterwards, rinse with water and remove any lingering hairs and crud with tweezers or toothpicks. Allow to dry.

ALL AROUND THE HOUSE

Wash your windows

Spray on a solution of equal parts vinegar and water. Polish with newspaper for a streak-free shine.

Remove tape or sticky residue on windows

Rub sticky area with warm vinegar, allow to soak in, and then peel or scrub off.

Clean no-wax floors

Make them shine with a solution of 1/2 cup of vinegar and a 1/2 gallon of warm water.

Clean indoor and outdoor carpet

Mix a gallon of water, a cup of vinegar and just enough dish soap to make sudsy. Brush it on the carpeting and blot dry with towels.

Clean brick floors and walls

Mop or brush them with a cup of vinegar mixed into a gallon of hot water.

Clean varnished or natural woodwork

Wipe down with a cloth moistened lightly with a solution of water and a few drops of vinegar.

Remove old glue from wood

Wipe area with hot vinegar.

Clean wood furniture

Make a solution of 1 tablespoon of vinegar to 1 quart of water. Wipe down furniture and dry with a lint-free cloth.

Peel off wallpaper

Spray the wallpaper with a solution of equal parts vinegar and water until it's saturated. Wait a few minutes and then scrape off.

Clean mini blinds

Make a solution of equal parts vinegar and hot water. Put on a cotton gardening glove, moisten your fingers in the vinegar solution, and slide your fingers across both slides of the slat. (Periodically wash off your glove in some clean water.)

Polish up the paneling

Combine 1 pint of warm water, 4 tablespoons of white vinegar, and 2 tablespoons of olive oil in a container. Cover tightly and mix together with a few vigorous shakes. Wipe down paneling with a cloth soaked in the mixture, then polish with a dry cloth.

Restore luster to leather furniture

In a spray bottle combine equals parts vinegar and boiled linseed oil. Shake it up to mix. Then spray it on your chair or other piece of furniture and spread evenly with a cloth. Let it sit for a few minutes and then rub if off with a clean cloth.

Cover up scratches in wood furniture

Mix vinegar and iodine together in a small container and apply to scratch with a small artist's brush. For darker woods, use more iodine; for lighter woods, use more vinegar.

Remove decals from surfaces

Brush with a couple of coats of vinegar. Allow to soak in. Decals should easily wash off after several minutes.

Clean stainless steel and chrome fixtures

Spray or wipe on a light coating of full-strength vinegar and polish to desired shine.

Clean eyeglasses

Wipe each lens with a drop of vinegar for a streak-free shine. (Don't use on plastic lenses.)

Clean book covers

Wipe with a cloth dampened in a solution of one part vinegar and two parts water.

Save a pair of scissors

Clean those sticky, grimy scissors by wiping the blades down with a cloth dampened with full-strength vinegar. Then polish to a nice gleam using a dry cloth. (Using water alone could lead to rust on the blades or the fastener holding the blades together.)

Freshen flowers

To each pint of water used, add a teaspoon each of vinegar and sugar. Will lengthen lives of fresh-cut flowers.

Get rid of gnats

In a small dish or cup, mix together equal parts apple cider vinegar and dish detergent, and set it out where the gnats are most problematic. The vinegar's sweet smell will attract them, and the dish soap will trap and kill them in the dish.

Remove smoke odors

Place a bowl of vinegar in a corner of a room to keep the room from becoming stale with cigarette smoke.

Clean deep vases

Pour a solution of vinegar and salt into the vase and let stand for an hour. Shake well and rinse thoroughly.

Brass cleaning, method 1

Mix a teaspoon of salt into a cup of vinegar. Add enough flour to make a thin paste. Rub onto the brass and allow to stand for 15 minutes. Rinse with warm water and dry to a polish.

Brass cleaning, method 2

Allow the object to soak overnight in a solution of vinegar and salt. Scrub the next morning with a brush, and wash in hot, soapy water. Rinse well.

Clean silver rings and other objects

Soak them in a solution of 1/2 cup of vinegar and 2 tablespoons of baking soda for two hours. Will make dull and dark rings look shiny and new.

Soften still paintbrushes

Boil brushes in equal parts vinegar and water for five minutes.

Get rid of paint odors

Place a small bowl of vinegar in a freshly painted room to absorb odors.

Dissolve rust from nuts and bolts

Soak the rusty objects in a bowl of full-strength vinegar. Brush away residue and dry.

Clean gold jewelry

Submerge solid gold jewelry items in a cup of apple cider vinegar for 15 minutes. Then dry with a soft cloth.

OUTSIDE IDEAS

Kill grass on walks and driveways

Pour vinegar directly on unwanted grass. (Be careful not to pour on wanted plants!)

Kill weeds

Spray full strength vinegar on tops of weeds. Reapply to new growth until weeds have been starved.

Increase soil acidity

In hard-water areas, add a cup of vinegar to a gallon of tap water for watering acid-loving plants like gardenias, azaleas, or rhododendrons. The vinegar releases iron into the soil for the plants to use.

Treat plant diseases

Vinegar is useful in treating many plant diseases such as black spot, rust, and powdery mildew. Mix 2 tablespoons of apple cider vinegar in 2 quarts of water, and pour into a spray bottle. Spray the solution on your diseased plants in the morning or early evening (when temperatures are cooler and there's less direct light) until the condition is cured.

Neutralize garden lime

Rinse your hands liberally with vinegar after working with garden lime to avoid rough and flaking skin.

Keep visitors out of your garden

Soak several rags in full-strength vinegar and hang on stakes around your garden. The smell of vinegar will deter many animals, including deer, racoons, rabbits, cats, and dogs. Resoak the rags every 7 to 10 days.

Deter ants

Spray vinegar under appliances, around door and window frames, and along other known ant trails.

Bid adieu to bird droppings

Spray or pour full-strength apple cider vinegar on the poo piles and wipe up with paper towels.

Clean a hummingbird feeder

Keep those birdies coming back by keeping their feeder free from sticky, crusted-on sugar water. Clean with a solution of equal parts apple cider vinegar and hot water, using a small brush if necessary. Rinse good with cold water and allow to dry completely in the sun before adding new food.

Keep your car windows frost-free

Coat the windows the night before with a solution of three parts vinegar to one part water.

Polish car chrome

Apply full-strength vinegar with a soft cloth and polish to desired shine.

Clean car carpets

Make a solution of equal parts water and vinegar and sponge into the carpet. Wait a few minutes and then blot up with paper towels or rags. This will also remove salt residue that accumulates over the winter months.

Remove bumper stickers

Repeatedly wipe full-strength vinegar over the bumper sticker until it's saturated. Try peeling off in a few minutes. May have to reapply the vinegar.

Prolong your propane

Soak new propane lantern wicks in vinegar for several hours. Let dry before using. Will burn longer and brighter.

Clean milking equipment

Rinse with vinegar to leave system clean, disinfected and deodorized without harmful chemical residue.

Keep chickens from pecking each other

Add a splash of apple cider vinegar to their drinking water.

Clean mold and mildew off patio furniture

Spray full-strength vinegar on the affected area. The stains should wipe off easily, and the vinegar will inhibit the mildew from growing back for a while.

Clean mold and mildew off wood decks and wood furniture

In a gallon of water, mix 1 cup of ammonia, 1/2 cup of vinegar, and 1/4 cup baking soda. Brush or sponge the affected areas, rinse with cold water, and allow to dry.

KIDS AND PETS

Clean baby bottles

Soak bottles in vinegar for several hours to clean and deodorize.

Wash baby clothes and diapers

Add a cup of vinegar to the rinse cycle to break down uric acid and soap residue. Will leave clothes soft and less likely to cause a rash.

Make child's clay

Mix 2 cups of flour and a cup of salt. Stir in a teaspoon of vinegar and a 1/2 cup of water. Knead until soft. Divide into smaller portions if desired and store in refrigerator.

Remove crayon and ink marks

Using a sponge or brush, apply full-strength vinegar to the marks and rub away.

Color Easter eggs

Mix 1 teaspoon of vinegar, 1/2 cup of hot water, and food coloring in a bowl deep enough to submerge an egg.

Make an erupting volcano

- *The Volcano* – Combine 6 cups of flour, 2 cups of salt, 4 tablespoons of cooking oil, and 2 cups of water. Mix until smooth and firm (add more water if needed). In a four-sided baking pan (so the "lava" stays contained), place a pop bottle upright and mold the dough around it into a volcano shape. Be careful not to cover the hole or drop dough into it.

- ***The Eruption*** – Fill the bottle most of the way full with warm water and a bit of red food coloring. Add 6 drops of dish detergent to the bottle. Add 2 tablespoons of baking soda next. Then slowly pour vinegar into the bottle and watch your volcano blow its top!

Remove skunk odor from a dog

Rub fur with a solution of 1 cup of vinegar to 2 gallons of water. Dry off the dog but don't rinse off the solution.

Prevent fleas, ticks and mange

Add a teaspoon of vinegar to 1 quart of your pet's drinking water. Alternatively, spray a solution of equal parts vinegar and water directly on your dog's fur and rub it in. (This is a little trickier with cats. They really don't like vinegar. See next tip.)

Keep cats away

Sprinkle vinegar on those areas you don't want them walking, sleeping or scratching on.

Clean pet urine from a carpet

Apply full-strength vinegar to the affected area. Blot with cold water and let dry.

COOKING TIPS

Make a buttermilk substitute

Add a tablespoon of vinegar to a cup of milk, stir it in, and let it stand for five minutes to thicken. Instant recipe fix!

Tenderize meat

For tough cuts of meat, make a marinade of 1/2 cup of vinegar (your choice as to taste) and 1 cup of heated liquid such as bouillon. Alternatively, add a tablespoon of white vinegar to your cooking liquids (for roasts, stew meats, etc.). Either way, the acetic acid in the vinegar breaks down the meat fibers, making them more tender and tasty.

Cook tastier fish

To give fish a tender, sweeter taste, soak it before cooking for 20 minutes in a mixture of 1 quart of water and 2 tablespoons of vinegar.

Freshen vegetables

Soak wilted vegetables in a quart of cold water and a tablespoon of vinegar. They'll spring up like new!

Keep potatoes white

Keep peeled potatoes from turning dark by putting them in pot of water (enough to cover) and adding 2 teaspoons of vinegar.

Make your own wine vinegar

Mix 2 tablespoons of vinegar with 1 teaspoon of dry red wine.

Replace a lemon

For normal taste buds, 1/4 teaspoon of vinegar equals 1 teaspoon of lemon juice. (Especially useful in fish recipes where you might want to cut down on odor and yet keep the taste.)

Firm up the gelatin in desserts

Add a teaspoon of vinegar for every box of gelatin used to keep those molded desserts from sagging in the summer heat.

Keep cheese longer

Wrap cheese in a vinegar-soaked cloth and keep it in a sealed container to lengthen its lifespan.

Boil better eggs

Add a tablespoon or two of vinegar to the water when boiling eggs to keep them from cracking and to allow for easier peeling.

Poach better eggs

Add a tablespoon of vinegar to the water when poaching eggs to coagulate the egg white and form a neat and compact shape to the finished product.

Prepare fluffier rice

Add a teaspoon of vinegar to the water when it boils. The rice will come out fluffier and not as sticky.

Make a simple salad dressing

Whisk together 1/4 cup of vinegar, 3/4 cup of olive oil, and a dash of Italian seasonings.

Dampen your appetite

Sprinkling a little vinegar on prepared food is said to take the edge off your appetite.

Boil better vegetables and beans

Add a teaspoon or two of vinegar to the water when boiling or steaming cauliflower, beets, and other vegetables and legumes. It will help them keep their color and reduce their gas-causing effects.

Make pasta less sticky

Add a splash of vinegar to the water as it cooks. Will also reduce the starch.

HEALTH AND HYGIENE

Soothe a bee or jellyfish sting

Mix three parts vinegar to one part water and apply to sting. Will soothe irritation and relieve itching. (WARNING: Do not apply vinegar to a Portuguese man-of-war sting. It could increase the amount of toxin released into the body.)

Relieve sunburn

Gently rub white or apple cider vinegar to skin. Apply as quickly as possible to stop the pain from getting too bad.

Condition hair

After shampooing, add a tablespoon of vinegar to your rinse to dissolve sticky residue left by shampoo.

Relieve dry and itchy skin

Add 1/2 cup of vinegar to your bath water. It will not only soften your skin, but will help keep your tub clean too.

Fight dandruff

An old folk remedy suggests warming apple cider vinegar, pouring it on the hair, and then wrapping a towel around the head. Let it set for an hour and then wash.

Eliminate underarm odor

Splash on some vinegar!

Freshen your breath

Dissolve 2 tablespoons of apple cider vinegar and 1 teaspoon of salt in a glass of warm water. Rinse with this solution to get rid of onion and garlic odors.

Polish nails with ease

Before applying polish, rub fingernails with vinegar-dipped cotton balls. Cleans the nails and helps polish stay on longer.

Clean dentures

Soak dentures overnight in undiluted white vinegar. Brush and rinse in the morning.

Ease heartburn

Mix 1 tablespoon of apple cider vinegar, 1/2 teaspoon of baking soda, and a dash of sugar in a glass of water. Drink the solution about an hour after eating.

Soothe a sore throat

Mix 1 teaspoon of vinegar with a glass of water and a little honey. Gargle first, then swallow. (If you want, you can skip the honey. Also remember: no honey for children under one year old.)

Treat a raw throat

Gargle with 1 tablespoon of apple cider vinegar and 1 teaspoon of salt dissolved in a glass of warm water. Repeat several times a day if needed for a throat left raw and sore from coughing or overuse.

Breathe easier

Add 1/4 cup of vinegar to your vaporizer the next time you're congested.

Pamper your feet

Soak your feet in a solution of vinegar and warm water nightly. Your feet will soon become noticeably softer, plus it helps fight toenail fungus.

Remove warts

Mix a cup of vinegar in some warm water. Soak the wart every day for 20 minutes it disappears.

Soak aching muscles

Add two cups of apple cider vinegar to your bath water. Hey, it tenderizes meat, right?

Relieve morning sickness

Drink apple cider vinegar mixed with water and a little honey to help calm a queasy stomach.

Treat skin burns

Apply ice-cold vinegar immediately to burn for relief and to prevent blisters. (Prepare ahead of time by keeping a bottle of vinegar in the refrigerator.)

Make a vinegar elixir

A teaspoon of apple cider vinegar in a glass of water, with a bit of honey added for flavor, will take the edge off your appetite and give you an overall healthy feeling. Try it as an afternoon pick-up and feel the difference!

A Word of Caution: While a teaspoon or two of apple cider vinegar is safe for most people, consult your doctor first if you are taking prescription medications, particularly diuretics and insulin, as the vinegar may interact negatively with these drugs and cause low potassium levels.

Also, don't think that just because one or two teaspoons is "good," more is better. Keep in mind that apple cider vinegar is highly acidic and could irritate your throat if taken in large quantities.

BLOOD SUGAR AND WEIGHT LOSS

Vinegar and Blood Glucose Control

The latest research shows that taking vinegar with a meal reduces the glucose response to a carbohydrate load in healthy adults as well as those suffering with type 2 diabetes. Based on these findings, researchers recommend taking two teaspoons of vinegar before or with your meals to reduce blood sugar levels. And no, you don't have to drink it straight. Here are some easy, tasty ways to get your daily dose of vinegar:

- Use a vinegar and oil dressing on your salads. Just be careful not to use a fruity or sweet vinegar; white, apple cider, balsamic, and red wine are all good choices. Also make sure your dressing is at least 50 to 75 percent vinegar. Add some Italian seasonings, minced garlic, or Dijon mustard for additional flavoring.

- Drizzle vinaigrette (or whatever dressing you just made for your salads) over steamed and roasted vegetables, such as cauliflower, broccoli, asparagus, and green beans.

- Dip your bread into a mixture of balsamic vinegar and olive oil. Be careful of the type of bread you use, as many grains will make blood sugar rise significantly. Sourdough is an excellent choice, as it contains a substance brought about by its fermentation process that tempers blood sugar levels.

- Marinate your meat and fish in vinegar. It's a natural tenderizer anyway, so your meat will come out tender, tasty, and moist.

- Eat pickles and other pickled vegetables with your meals. Korean kimchi and German sauerkraut, for example, are good vinegar-rich vegetable side dishes.

Vinegar and Weight Control

Can vinegar help you lose weight? The answer is . . . likely, possibly, maybe.

As I've just mentioned, current research clearly demonstrates that vinegar helps control the glycemic effect of carbohydrate-laden meals. Now, in weight loss circles it is pretty widely acknowledged that a low-glycemic diet often results in weight loss. So a logical deduction would be that, yes, vinegar can help you lose weight since it induces a lower-GI effect.

The problem is, there aren't any definitive scientific studies out there yet that prove this in particular. There are, however, plenty of anecdotal weight loss results that have come about from other studies examining vinegar's effects on cholesterol, appetite suppression, and fat deposits.

Case in point: In 2004, Dr. Carol Johnston, a nutrition professor at the University of Arizona, conducted a study to examine the effects of vinegar on cholesterol levels. While Johnston found the vinegar to have no effect on lowering cholesterol, she did discover, unintentionally, that those who ingested a tablespoon of vinegar before lunch and dinner lost an average of two pounds over four weeks. (And this was accomplished during the holiday months of November and December.)

In 2005, a study conducted by Swedish researcher Dr. Elin Ostman found participants to be less hungry a couple of hours after eating bread with vinegar as opposed to eating bread alone. Folklorists have long maintained that vinegar acts as an appetite suppressant (and therefore a weight loss aid). Science now seems to correlate this.

More recently, a 2009 Japanese study was conducted on mice in which one group of mice was fed a high-fat diet and acetic acid (the main component in vinegar), and another group of mice was fed the same diet but given water instead of acetic acid. After six weeks, the mice in the acetic acid group had 10% less body fat than the mice in the water group.

The Japanese researchers believe that acetic acid activates genes that produce proteins that in turn help the body break down fats. Such an action helps prevent fat buildup and thus helps guard against weight gain.

Dr. Johnston attributes these results to another unique function of acetic acid. She describes acetic acid as basically a starch and sugar blocker. It inhibits the activity of various carbohydrate-digesting enzymes, such as amylase, sucrase, maltase, and lactase. When these enzymes are blocked, sugars and starches pass through the digestive tract much the way that indigestible fiber does.

Much more research is needed to definitively proclaim vinegar as a weight loss wonder, despite the claims of many fad diet proponents and books. But given its proven effect on blood glucose, tempering the glycemic load of carbohydrate-rich meals, appetite suppression, and key metabolic processes, it only seems natural to include it in one's daily health regime.

Did you catch that key word? *Natural*. Vinegar is all that and more.

Last Words

Needless to say, this compilation is by no means exhaustive. Perhaps after reading through, you've come up with some of your own ideas for using vinegar, based on your personal needs. After all, if vinegar can, say, deodorize a lunchbox, maybe it can also deodorize your . . . (fill in the blank). Feel free to experiment. The secret to mastering household tasks, obtaining better health, and keeping the planet greener is only a bottle away!

ACKNOWLEDGEMENTS

A myriad of resources was consulted in compiling this compendium of vinegar lore and facts. While too numerous and impractical to list individually, the author would like to offer a special acknowledgement to The Vinegar Institute, an international trade association representing the vast majority of vinegar manufacturers and bottlers. The Vinegar Institute is an invaluable source for all things vinegar, and especially for keeping up on the latest research news and market trends. You can visit online at http://www.versatilevinegar.org.

The author would also like to acknowledge the following sources for the information used in the discussions of glucose control and weight loss:

Challem, Jack. "A Spoonful of Vinegar Helps the Blood Sugar Go Down." Dlife.com. 23 June 2011.

Johnston, Carol S., and Cindy A. Gass. "Vinegar: Medicinal Uses and Antiglycemic Effect." Medscape.com. 30 May 2006.

Kondo, Tomoo, et al. "Acetic Acid Upregulates the Expression of Genes for Fatty Acid Oxidation Enzymes in Liver To Suppress Body Fat Accumulation." Journal of Agricultural and Food Chemistry, 2009, 57 (13), pp 5982–5986.

Ostman E, Granfeldt Y, Persson L, et al. "Vinegar Supplementation Lowers Glucose and Insulin Responses and Increases Satiety After a Bread Meal in Healthy Subjects." European Journal of Clinical Nutrition, 2005, 59, 983-988.

Baking Soda Solutions

Economical, Eco-Friendly Ideas for Your House, Your Yard and You

By M.B. Ryther

Copyright 2012 M.B. Ryther
All rights reserved.

BAKING SODA 101

The Multi-Purpose "Power Powder"

Every cook knows that baking soda is a needed ingredient for cakes, cookies, muffins, breads, and other baked goods. And many of us keep a little orange box in the back of the frig to cut down on food odors. But have you ever thought about using baking soda to relieve itchy skin? Or to freshen your dog's breath? How about adding a pinch to fluff up your mashed potatoes? Or to soften your clothes? Got dirty pots and pans? Got bored kids? Got a fire?! Let baking soda come to the rescue!

Yes, baking soda can do all of that and much more. That lonely little box of white powder sitting in your kitchen cupboard is actually a powerful chemical agent that can be used to clean, deodorize, sanitize, and solve various problems all around your house and yard. Non-toxic and environmentally friendly, it's safe to use inside and outside, around the pets and kids, even on the pets and kids. A small box is cheaper than a candy bar and can do your body a whole lot more good. As versatile and effective as baking soda is, it's a wonder the stuff isn't sold by the crate!

A Short History

The discovery and development of baking soda can be traced back to American colonial times. In the mid-eighteenth century, colonists used a crude potassium carbonate substance extracted from wood ash called potash as an ingredient for making soap and glass. Potash production soon became a major industry, with large amounts of potash being exported to England for use in factories. In the 1760s bakers, by chance, discovered that adding pearlash (concentrated potash) to sourdough not only sweetened the dough because of its alkalinity, but made it rise by interacting with the dough's acids and producing carbon dioxide bubbles. This discovery revolutionized baking and increased even more the demand for pearlash on both sides of the Atlantic.

The American Revolution, however, coupled with diminishing European forests, prompted Europe to look for other sources of carbonates. In 1783 the French Academy of Sciences ran a contest for inventors who could develop a process for converting salt (sodium chloride) to soda ash (sodium carbonate). French chemist Nicolas LeBlanc won the prize in 1791 for reacting salt with sulfuric acid, coal, and limestone to produce soda ash. So now, not only did Europe have its own plentiful supply of sodium carbonate to replace the expensive imported American potassium carbonates, but the soda ash was found by bakers to be just as good a leavening agent as potash.

Medical researchers played the next important role in baking soda's development. European chemists bubbled carbon dioxide gas through solutions of sodium carbonate to create sodium bicarbonate, a less alkaline compound that could be used to safely soothe stomach acids. Over in America, in 1846, an upstate New York doctor named Austin Church discovered a different way to produce sodium bicarbonate from sodium carbonate using heat. The process was so successful that Dr. Church went into business with his brother-in-law, John Dwight, to mass produce this new, high-grade sodium bicarbonate. They moved their business to New York City to take advantage of the ports there and called their product baking soda.

In 1865, Dr. Church retired from John Dwight & Company, and then two years later helped his two sons found a new business, Church & Company. They chose as their company symbol a red circle containing the arm of Vulcan–the Roman god of fire and metallurgy–holding a raised hammer and called their main product Arm & Hammer Bicarbonate of Soda. Though the two families competed in the same business, relations remained friendly, and in 1896 the descendants of both company founders merged their businesses to form Church & Dwight, Co., using the Arm & Hammer trademark. Today, Church & Dwight control 90 percent of the consumer baking soda market.

Where It Comes from Today

Today all baking soda in North America is mined from the mineral trona, the largest deposit of which exists in Green River, Wyoming. Trona is composed of sodium bicarbonate and sodium carbonate. The ore is removed from the mines, crushed, rinsed, and heated to produce sodium carbonate. The sodium carbonate is then dissolved in water and carbon dioxide is forced through the solution, releasing sodium bicarbonate crystals. The crystals are washed, dried, and packaged as baking soda.

Interestingly, sodium bicarbonate is also produced naturally in the human body, its main purpose being to help maintain the acidity (pH) level of the blood. It also helps neutralize stomach acids so we aren't inundated with ulcers; it assists in our breathing by transporting carbon dioxide from tissue to the lungs for disposal; and, being present in saliva, it neutralizes plaque acids which could otherwise dissolve our teeth.

Why and Where It Works

Baking soda has a unique dual chemical nature that allows it to interact with both acids and bases. Slightly alkaline itself, baking soda acts as a neutralizing base in the presence of an acid; and it acts as a neutralizing acid in the presence of a base. These properties are what make baking soda so useful in so many different situations. For example, the strong smells of sour milk, an acidic odor, and spoiled fish, a basic odor, both can be neutralized by chemically reacting with baking soda.

Baking soda is an effective surface cleaner as well because of its ability to take on different forms to match the job at hand. Greasy pots and pans? Baking soda's alkaline nature interacts with the fatty acids in grease and dirt to make a soap. Need a gentle scouring powder? Sprinkle some baking soda on a sponge and wipe away. Or make a paste with a little added water and apply with a brush. Baking soda is gentle enough that it won't scratch most household surfaces, yet powerful enough to break up dirt, stains, and sticky residues. If a little extra "boost" is needed for a particularly tough job, add baking soda to soap or detergent, or mix it with vinegar (an acid) to produce effervescent bubbles that will effectively lift dirt from most surfaces.

Perhaps the number one reason to have a box of baking soda in your kitchen is for its fire extinguishing properties. Thrown at the base of a grease or electrical fire, baking soda will smother the flames quickly and effectively. (Baking soda is NOT recommended for fires involving paper, wood, cloth, and plastics, as these substances could reignite. Use water instead.) As further testimony to baking soda's effectiveness, most commercial fire extinguishers contain sodium bicarbonate.

As discussed earlier, sodium bicarbonate is produced in the human body, so not surprisingly baking soda has many medicinal and biological uses too. Many prescription and over-the-counter drugs contain it, and, as you'll read about later in this book, there are a myriad of other health and hygiene uses for baking soda, ranging from acid indigestion to stuffy noses.

The largest commercial use of baking soda in North America may come as a surprise: cattle feed. To reduce stomach acid in cows, and thereby increasing milk production, baking soda is mixed into the cows' feed. It is advantageous to beef cattle as well by allowing the steers to maintain their maximum weight gain. Too much acid in a steer's rumen (partially digested food) decreases the animal's feed intake, efficiency, and weight gain. Sodium bicarbonate is also added to chicken feed to produce tougher egg shells.

Lest we forget, baking soda is also great for . . . baking! Again, it all comes down to chemistry. Baking soda's ability to make doughy mixtures rise is due to its reaction with the acid in things such as chocolate, milk, yogurt, vinegar, and lemon juice. It neutralizes the acid and causes carbon dioxide bubbles to be released. The bubbles get trapped by the gluten (the protein in wheat flour) and cause the mixture to rise.

That's the overview of baking soda's prowess and practicality. Now it's time to get down to the details and explore all the ways that baking soda can work for you.

Using Baking Soda

Baking soda is generally used in one of four forms:

1. Open box (for deodorizing spaces). Just remove the top from a box of baking soda or make a "soda sachet" or other decorative deodorizer as described later in this book.

2. Dry (sprinkled right from the box or applied to a damp sponge).

3. Paste (3 parts baking soda to 1 part water, or just enough liquid to create a paste).

4. Solution (4 tablespoons baking soda dissolved in 1 quart of warm water).

Don't get too hung up on exact measurements. Use the given suggestions as a guideline at first, and adjust when and if you feel it's necessary. Often times a "pinch" or a "shake" is just as good as hauling out the measuring spoon. The exception to this is with certain health and hygiene uses such as taking baking soda as an antacid. Be sure to follow those guidelines carefully, as taking too much or at the wrong times could cause serious health problems.

A Few Recommendations

- Test your baking soda's freshness by adding 1/4 teaspoon of baking soda to a tablespoon of vinegar. If it bubbles, it's still good.

- Use a grated cheese container to keep your baking soda in. The holes makes sprinkling easy, and if you need more powder, just untwist the cap.

- As a deodorizer, baking soda works best when kept in a more confined space. It is also more effective the longer it is in contact with the odor.

- Keep a box of baking soda handy where fires could occur, e.g., near the stove, by the grill, in the shop.

- Keep a box of baking soda in your emergency preparedness kits. Keep one in your car too.

- Test health and hygiene formulas on a small patch of skin–the inside of your arm, for example– before using if you're concerned about allergies or other sensitivities.

- As a time-saving shortcut, consider using a commercial-brand baking soda toothpaste for many of the jobs described in this book. For best results, use a paste rather than a gel, as the pastes contain more baking soda.

KITCHEN AID

Keep your refrigerator smelling fresh

Place an opened box of baking soda on a shelf and replace it every three months. Pour the expired soda down the kitchen drain or garbage disposal and freshen those up as well.

Clean big appliances

Remove stains, films, and stuck-on food by wiping down your big appliances with baking soda sprinkled on a damp sponge. Rinse off and dry.

Clean and deodorize the microwave

Boil a solution of 2 tablespoons of baking soda and 1 cup of water in the microwave for a few minutes. Then easily wipe off all the grime.

Clean the blender

Fill the blender half full with water. Add 1 teaspoon of baking soda and 1 drop of liquid dish detergent. Place the lid on tightly and turn on the blender briefly. Rinse clean.

Make a gentle scouring powder

Blend 1 cup of baking soda and 1 cup of salt together. Store in a covered container. Apply with a damp sponge.

Power up your dish soap

Boost the grease-cutting power of your liquid soap by adding baking soda to your hot, soapy water. Use 2 tablespoons to a cup, depending upon the volume of water. Hand wash your dishes as usual. For tough stains, sprinkle baking soda directly on the affected area and scour with a scrubber.

Clean the kitchen sink

Sprinkle baking soda into sink and add a little vinegar. As it bubbles, scrub with a brush and rinse. Or simply wipe down the sink with baking soda sprinkled on a damp sponge. Baking soda is a terrific nonabrasive cleanser for stainless steel sinks.

Freshen up smelly sponges and dishcloths

After washing dishes in your powered-up dish water, let your sponge or dishcloth soak in the baking soda and water for a while before rinsing the sink out. Alternatively, soak your cleaning sponges and rags in a solution of 4 tablespoons of baking soda and 1 quart of warm water to get them clean and odor-free.

Clean the coffee maker

Fill reservoir with a solution of 4 tablespoons of baking soda per quart of water. Run the coffee maker through one cycle. Repeat with one to two additional cycles of plain water. Clean the exterior with a baking soda solution or pure baking soda sprinkled on a damp sponge.

Clean the coffeepot

Wash glass and stainless steel coffeepots and teapots with a baking soda solution (4 tablespoons of soda in 1 quart of water). For badly stained pots, use hot water to make the solution and let it sit in the coffeepot for an hour. Or scrub with a baking soda paste (3 parts baking soda to 1 part water).

Control dishwasher odors

Sprinkle baking soda on the bottom between loads.

Drain cleaner 1 (strong)

Combine 2 cups of baking soda and 2 cups of salt. Mix well and store in an airtight container. Periodically pour 1 cup of mixture down the drain followed by 1 quart of boiling water. Let sit for several hours or overnight, then flush with hot tap water for at least a minute.

Drain cleaner 2 (stronger)

Pour 1/2 cup of baking soda down the drain followed by 1/2 cup of white vinegar. Let sit for about 2 hours. Flush with hot tap water for at least one minute. (If drain is clogged, use up to a cup of both baking soda and vinegar, and repeat as necessary.) Also good for the garbage disposal.

Remove odors from surfaces

To rid wood and other porous surfaces of garlic, onion, and other strong food odors, wipe the area down with baking soda sprinkled on a damp sponge. Rinse with water.

Camouflage countertop cuts

Small cuts in your countertop will seem less conspicuous when kept clean with a paste of baking soda and water.

Remove odors from your hands

Neutralize garlic, onion, and fish smells on your hands by sprinkling baking soda in the palm of one hand, adding enough water to make a paste, rubbing your hands together well, rinsing and drying.

Clean and deodorize cutting boards

Scrub with a paste of 3 parts baking soda per 1 part water. Rinse well and dry. If particularly odorous, let the paste sit on the board for about 10 minutes before rinsing. For deep periodic cleanings, sprinkle baking soda generously over the surface of the board, then dribble liberally with vinegar. After the bubbling subsides, rinse with hot water.

Clean glass stovetops

Clean with either a baking soda solution or a paste depending on how dirty the surface is. Use a small brush for getting into the corners. For burned-on splatters, first wet the area with water and then sprinkle a generous amount of baking soda over the surface. Let it sit for a while before wiping up. Repeat if necessary.

Clean glass oven doors

Sprinkle baking soda onto grimy oven or toaster oven doors, cover with wet paper towels and let stand for a while. Then wipe the glass clean with a damp sponge or cloth.

Take care of oven spills

Clean major oven spills by sprinkling them with baking soda while they're still fresh. Let them set for a while, and then wipe up with warm soapy water and a sponge.

Extinguish stove fires

Turn off burner or broiler and toss handfuls of baking soda on the flames. Water is ineffective on a grease fire and will only spread it.

Clean wire mesh filters on range hoods

Set them in a sink or pan of hot water. Pour on a generous amount of baking soda. Scrubbing them clean will be much easier.

Clean oven and grill racks

Put the racks in a plastic garbage bag, preferably outside. Mix 1 cup of baking soda and 1/2 cup of ammonia and pour over the racks. Tie the bag up and let it set overnight. The racks should wipe clean in the morning. (If you don't want to mess around with ammonia, lay the racks on the ground outside, sprinkle with baking soda and leave them overnight. The next day scrub them with hot water.)

Clean the oven (elbow grease method)

[Note: *Not for self-cleaning models.*]

Make a paste of 3 parts baking soda per 1 part water. Scrub hard using a nylon scrubber. For tough jobs, use equal parts baking soda and salt in the paste. (In electric ovens, try not to get any of the paste on the heating elements. It could corrode them when they turn on.)

Clean the oven (ammonia method)

Set a cup of ammonia in the oven, close the door, and leave it there overnight. In the morning, take out the ammonia and sprinkle baking soda all over the oven surfaces. Wipe with wet paper towels. Most of the grime should come off. (Again, not for self-cleaning models.)

Clean the cookware

Shake a liberal amount of baking soda on a dirty pan, add a little dish detergent and hot water, and let sit for about 15 minutes. Then wash away the grime.

[Note: *For this and the following tips on cleaning various pots and pans, be aware that baking soda can darken aluminum cookware.*]

Remove burnt-on food from pots and pans

Cover the surface of the cookware with baking soda, add hot water and let it soak for 10 minutes.
Then scrub with more baking soda applied to a damp sponge. For tough jobs, bring to a boil 2 inches of water in the pan, remove from the heat, add 1/2 cup of baking soda, and let the pan sit overnight. In the morning it should clean easily with a sponge or, if needed, a nylon scrubber.

Remove grease and oil stains from pots and pans

Add the following ingredients to pots and pans that have a grease and oil buildups:

- 2 tablespoons baking soda
- 1/2 cup white vinegar
- 1 cup water

Boil the mixture in the pot for 10 minutes. Provide adequate ventilation for the vinegar fumes. Then wash as usual.

Clean roasting pans and bakeware

Baked-on foods, oils, and grease will come off much easier with this method: Liberally coat the surface with baking soda. Then combine 1/4 cup of vinegar with 3/4 cup of hot water and pour it over the soda. After the fizzling ebbs, wash as usual. This also works well with bakeware that has a buildup of cooking spray residue.

Shine the silverware

Make a paste of 3 parts baking soda to 1 part warm water. Apply to silver with a sponge. Rub, rinse, and buff dry.

Make crystal sparkle

Bring out the sparkle in your good crystal by giving it a short soak in baking soda and warm water.

Remove coffee and tea stains

Sprinkle baking soda directly on the stained cup, pot or dish, and scour with a damp sponge. For tough stains, soak overnight in a solution of 1/4 cup of baking soda in 1 quart of warm water.

Deodorize glass and plastic food containers

Add two tablespoons baking soda and fill container with hot water. Cover and shake. Allow to sit for a couple of hours. For strong odors, allow to soak overnight.

Clean thermoses and water bottles

Fill with water and 1 or 2 tablespoons of baking soda. Let sit for a couple of hours and then rinse out the solution with hot water. (A dash of lemon juice or vinegar will also help clean off coffee stains.)

Control garbage odors

Neutralize kitchen garbage can odors by sprinkling baking soda in the bottom of the can before inserting a plastic bag. You can also sprinkle the soda on the bottom of the bag itself, as well as sprinkling it in along with added trash.

Remove heel and scuff marks

Remove marks from linoleum or vinyl floors with baking soda on a damp sponge.

Clean the kitchen floor

Mop no-wax and tile floors with a solution of 1/2 cup of baking soda in a bucket of warm water.

COOKING TIPS

Fluff up omelettes

Add 1/2 teaspoon of baking soda for every 3 eggs to make a fluffy omelette.

Make fluffier mashed potatoes

Add a pinch of baking soda to your potatoes during mashing.

Stop gravy from separating

When cooking gravy, add a pinch or two of baking soda to emulsify the fat globules.

Prevent syrup from crystallizing

Add a pinch of baking soda to any syrup while it's boiling.

Prevent milk from curdling

Keep milk from curdling during boiling by adding a pinch of baking soda.

Tenderize meat

Rub tough meat with baking soda. Let it sit for a couple of hours, rinse and cook.

Get rid of fishy flavor

Soak the uncooked fish in 2 tablespoons of baking soda and 1 quart of water for at least a half hour. Rinse and pat dry before cooking.

Get rid of gamey taste

To remove or minimize the "wild" taste in game meat, soak the uncooked meat in baking soda and water overnight in the refrigerator or a cooler. Rinse and pat dry before cooking.

Clean and sanitize fruits and vegetables

Remove dirt and residue from fresh fruits and vegetables by scrubbing them with baking soda sprinkled on a wet sponge. Rinse with water.

Make veggies less bitter

Remove the bitter taste of turnips, mustard greens, and other bitter vegetables by adding 1/2 teaspoon of baking soda to the cooking water.

Cook better cauliflower

Add 1 teaspoon of baking soda to the cooking water to keep cauliflower looking white while cutting down on its odor.

Cut the acid in tomato-based sauces

Add a pinch of baking soda to a pot of spaghetti sauce or chili to bring down the acidity level.

Cut the acid in coffee

Love coffee but not the afterburn? Add a pinch of baking soda to a cup of your regular coffee. It will tone down the acid but not the taste.

Make a fun, fizzy drink

Stir a 1/4 teaspoon of baking soda into a glass of orange juice, grapefruit juice or lemonade to make a fun, fizzy drink for children (or adults). The soda will also cut down the acidity level.

Prevent cloudy ice tea

Add a pinch of baking soda to the mixture. It will also tone down any bitterness.

Balance out the vinegar

If you've added too much vinegar to a dish, add a pinch of baking soda to counteract the excess acidity.

LAUNDRY SOLUTIONS

Power up your laundry detergent

Add 1/2 cup of baking soda to your liquid detergent load to make clothes softer, cleaner, whiter, and brighter. [Note: this only works with liquid detergents.]

Replace your fabric softener

Add 1/2 cup of baking soda to your rinse cycle instead of fabric softener. Family members who have sensitive skin will thank you. (This also takes the chlorine smell out of towels.)

Brighten whites

Add 1/4 cup to 1/2 cup of baking soda to your regular amount of liquid chlorine bleach to get your white clothes even whiter.

Save on bleach

Get your clothes just as clean with less bleach odor by decreasing the amount of liquid bleach you use by half and substituting baking soda instead. Here's a basic formula: If you normally use 1 cup of bleach, add 1/2 cup of baking soda and cut the bleach to 1/2 cup. (Use less for front loading machines, e.g., 1/4 cup baking soda.)

Treat ring-around-the-collar

Before washing, treat dirty collars and cuffs with a paste of 3 parts baking soda to 2 parts white vinegar.

Make a pre-wash paste

Make a thick paste of 4 tablespoons baking soda and 1/4 cup warm water. Rub the paste onto food and perspiration stains before washing. For tough stains, allow the paste to set for a couple of hours.

Neutralize acid spills and stains

Acidic spills on clothing (drain openers, toilet bowl cleaners, battery acid, vomit, and urine) need to be flushed immediately with cold water and sprinkled with baking soda to neutralize the effect. Even if the acid has dried on the garment, sprinkle it with baking soda before washing. Otherwise the wash water will reactivate the acid, which will then continue to damage the article of clothing.

Pretreat smelly clothes

Soak clothes for an hour or more in a solution of 1/2 cup of baking soda and a gallon of warm water. Launder as normal.

Deodorize clothes before wash day

Keep odors at bay on work and athletic clothes that you can't wash right away. Sprinkle baking soda liberally into the pile of clothes. When they are ready to be washed, toss them in the machine, baking soda included.

Dechlorinate your swimsuits

Add a tablespoon of baking soda to a sink full of water and soak your swimming suits in it for a while. The chlorine will rinse away.

Clean your iron

Get rid of starch buildup and other residue from the bottom of an iron by rubbing it with a baking soda paste. (Make sure the iron is cool!) Then clean the steam holes with a dampened cotton swab dipped in baking soda.

Freshen the hamper

Sprinkle baking soda between the layers of clothes. When it's wash time, the clothes will have an added softener too.

Clean suede

Sprinkle baking soda on the dirty area and rub it in gently with a soft brush. Let it sit for about 15 minutes and then brush off. The baking soda will clean the dirt and absorb grease and odors.

Get unknotted

Sprinkle baking soda on a knotted cord or shoelace for easier untangling.

Deodorize smelly shoes

Sweeten smelly sneakers and other shoes by sprinkling a little baking soda inside. Shake out before wearing.

BATHROOM BENEFITS

Clean the toilet bowl

For routine maintenance, toss in 1/2 cup of baking soda and scour with toilet brush. Let sit for 5 minutes before flushing. For tough stains, pour in a 1/2 cup of baking soda and a 1/2 cup of vinegar and then scrub with toilet brush.

Treat the septic tank

Flush a cup of baking soda down the toilet once a week. (Make sure to do this on a regular basis, because every time new material enters the tank, the dissolved sodium bicarbonate is forced out.)

Clean the toilet tank

Pour half a box of baking soda into the toilet tank each month and let sit overnight. Flush in the morning for a clean tank and bowl.

Clean green

Avoid strong chemical-based bathroom cleaners by wiping down all your bathroom surfaces with baking soda on a damp sponge. Effective and safe to use on countertops, sinks, tubs, showers, chrome and stainless steel fixtures, porcelain, fiberglass, backsplashes, and tile.

Unplug the drains

Dissolve hair and scum from sink and tub drains with this mixture:

- 1 cup baking soda
- 1 cup salt
- 1/2 cup white vinegar
- 2 quarts boiling water

Pour the baking soda, salt and vinegar down the drain. Allow it to work for about 15 minutes. Then flush the drain with the boiling water, followed by hot tap water for one minute.

Prevent bathtub rings

Add 2 tablespoons of baking soda to your bath water. No more ring-around-the-tub, and your bath water will be softer too.

Clean the grout and tile

Make a paste of 3 parts baking soda per 1 part water. Apply to grout with an old toothbrush, and to tile with a damp sponge. Rinse after scrubbing. For tough stains, substitute bleach for the water. Rinse thoroughly. (Make sure to wear rubber gloves and provide ventilation while working with bleach.)

Clean the shower head

Fill a sturdy sandwich-sized plastic bag with 1/4 cup of baking soda and 1 cup of vinegar. Attach it around a scummy showerhead with a rubber band. Let it bubble and brew for an hour. Then remove the bag and turn on the water for a minute or so. Rinse and buff the showerhead to your liking.

Clean the shower doors

First spray the doors with white vinegar and let it set for a few minutes. Then scour with baking soda on a damp sponge. Rinse and wipe dry.

Clean the shower curtain

Slimy, grimy mildewed plastic shower curtains can usually be cleaned right in the washing machine. Add 1/2 cup of baking soda along with your regular detergent, and two bath towels for friction.

Run the machine on the gentle wash cycle. Then add 1 to 2 cups of vinegar to the rinse cycle. Put it in the dryer on low heat for a couple of minutes, then hang and let air dry.

Clean a fiberglass tub

Sprinkle baking soda all over the tub. Then take a cloth that's been soaked in vinegar and rub the surfaces clean. Rinse well. (Try this with fiberglass shower stalls too.)

Make a powerful soap scum cleanser

Mix together 1/4 cup of baking soda, 1/2 cup of vinegar, 1 cup of ammonia, and 1 gallon of warm water. Wearing rubber gloves, use a brush or sponge to apply the solution liberally to scummy shower walls and doors. Rinse well.

[Note: *Never mix chlorine bleach with ammonia. The combination can produce dangerous fumes!*]

Make a bathroom air freshener

Pour some baking soda into a decorative dish and leave on top of the toilet tank or on the floor behind the toilet. Replace every few weeks.

Clean the bathroom floor

Mop it up with a solution of 1/2 cup of baking soda in a bucket of warm water. Your floor will sparkle and your whole bathroom will smell fresh.

NURSERY HELP

Clean and deodorize diaper pails

Sprinkle a cup of baking soda on the bottom of the diaper pail before putting in the liner, or on the bottom of the liner itself. Sprinkle some in after each dirty diaper too. For more thorough cleanings, add a cup of baking soda to the empty pail and fill it with warm water. Let the solution sit for a couple of hours, then rinse and dry.

Clean and deodorize bottles

Get rid of sour milk and other odors by filling the bottles with hot water and a teaspoon of baking soda. Shake, rinse and clean as usual with a brush or cloth. For extra cleaning, soak the bottles, rings and nipples for several hours or overnight in a solution of 4 tablespoons baking soda per quart of warm water. Then wash and rinse as usual.

Blot bibs

Neutralize acidic spit-ups by promptly rubbing with dry baking soda. Also helps cut down on odors.

Sweeten and soften cloth diapers

Freshen by soaking in a solution of ½ cup baking soda and 2 quarts warm water.

Wash baby clothes

Clean stained baby clothes by adding 1/2 cup of baking soda to your wash water along with liquid laundry detergent. Deodorize by adding a 1/2 cup to the rinse cycle.

Clean high chairs, changing tables, car seats, and baby toys

Scrub with a solution of 4 tablespoons baking soda and 1 quart of warm water. For really tough jobs, scrub directly with baking soda on a damp sponge, rinse and dry.

Put a charge in old toys

Make a paste of baking soda and water and apply it to the contact points in the battery compartments of worn-out toys, flashlights, etc., to clean corrosion and renew connections.

"Dust" the stuffed animals

Periodically place your child's stuffed animals in a large plastic bag with ½ cup of baking soda. Shake vigorously. Let animals sit for 15 minutes, then brush baking soda off with a hairbrush. They'll look cleaner and smell fresher!

Soften baby's bath water

Toss a handful (approx. 1/2 cup) of baking soda into your baby's bath water. Minimizes the need for soap and soothes mild diaper rash.

Lower a high temperature

Similarly, putting a feverish baby into a bath of lukewarm water to which baking soda has been added can help lower the child's temperature.

Neutralize spit up

Make a solution of equal parts baking soda and water. For optimal use, keep it in a small squeeze bottle. When baby spits up, squirt the spot and blot it up before it gets too absorbed in clothing.

Treat cradle cap

First apply baby oil to the scalp, then rub baking soda into the oily hair. With a fine-toothed comb, gently dislodge the loose, flaky skin. Shampoo and rinse clean.

Counteract vomit

Mitigate the smell until you can clean it up by covering it with baking soda. (This will also help alert others as to where it's safe to step.)

Sweeten smelly feet

After drying your child's footed pajamas, sprinkle a little baking soda into the feet to keep the tootsies smelling fresh.

Clean up nighttime accidents

Remove all linens and sprinkle baking soda over the wet part of the mattress. Allow it to sit and soak up the moisture and odor. After it's dry, vacuum up the baking soda. Wash the linens with added baking soda to neutralize the smells.

Erase crayon marks

Remove them from walls by sprinkling baking soda on a damp sponge and rubbing over the area gently. (Also works good on pencil, marker, and grease marks.)

Polish baby shoes

Polish white baby shoes by rubbing with baking soda on a damp sponge. Rinse and lightly buff.

ALL AROUND THE HOUSE

Freshen upholstery

Generously sprinkle baking soda on upholstered furniture and let it sit for 15 minutes or so before vacuuming. Will eliminate smoke, food, and other odors.

Clean vinyl furniture

Wipe down with either a baking soda solution or baking soda sprinkled on a damp sponge. Will remove harmful grease and oils. For tough stains, scrub with a paste of 3 parts baking soda, 1 part water, and a few drops of dishwashing soap. Rinse with clean water and wipe dry.

Made a sachet

Make an allergy-free "soda sachet" by putting 1/3 cup or less of baking soda in the middle of a 6-inch circle of fabric, tissue, or a coffee filter. Gather the top and secure with a ribbon, a rubber band, or a twist tie. Alternatively, fill a small plastic container or cardboard box with baking soda, punch holes in the top, and set it where needed. (Of course, you can poke holes in a plain old box of baking soda and set that out as well.)

Clean mops and rags

First rinse the dirt out of them and then soak the mops and rags in a solution of 4 tablespoons of baking soda to 1 quart of water to get rid of residual smells. Rinse with clean water and set out to dry.

Renew sponges and scrub brushes

Same principle as above. Try soaking them overnight in a baking soda solution for best results.

Slip easily into rubber gloves

Pour baking soda into the fingers of the gloves. Your hands will end up smelling good too.

Clean fireplace bricks

Make a baking soda solution (4 tablespoons baking soda per 1 quart of warm water) and scrub the bricks with a brush.

Make marble tops look marvelous

Sprinkle baking soda on a damp sponge and apply to stained marble on furniture tops. Let the paste sit a few minutes before rinsing with water and drying.

Put your vase to work

In addition to providing a handy base substance for artificial flowers, baking soda in a vase also allows you to place a pretty deodorizer in the setting of your choice (such as bathrooms and kitty litter corners).

Enhance your humidifier

Add 2 tablespoons of baking soda to the water in your humidifier to get rid of musty odors.

Vanish vacation vapors

Sprinkle baking soda down sink drains, in tubs and showers, and in the toilets before leaving on vacation. This will prevent being greeted by stale odors when you get home.

Deodorize musty books

Make sure the book is thoroughly dry. Then sprinkle a little baking soda between the pages. Brush out after several days.

Freshen closets

Keep an opened box of baking soda (or a "soda sachet" as described previously) in your closets to absorb odors. Periodically sprinkle baking soda on the closet floor and let it sit overnight. Vacuum it up in the morning. (And don't forget to sprinkle some in your shoes!)

Banish paint and varnish smells

Leave open boxes of baking soda in your house, shop or garage to minimize paint and varnish smells.

Polish chrome and stainless steel, silver, and gold plating

Gently rub with baking soda on a damp sponge. (Not for use on decorative aluminum, or lacquered brass, bronze, or copper.)

Wash the walls

Clean washable walls with a solution of 1 cup of baking soda and 1 tablespoon of gentle dishwashing liquid mixed into a gallon of hot water.

Shampoo the carpet

Mix 1/2 cup of baking soda into 1 gallon of warm water and use the solution in a carpet cleaning machine. Or mix it in a bucket and scrub the carpet by hand with a brush. For stained areas, sprinkle a small amount on the stain while the carpet is damp and let it sit for a while before wiping up with a cloth or sponge. (It's a good idea to test for colorfastness first by applying a small amount of baking soda on an inconspicuous piece of the carpet.)

Deodorize the carpet (dry method)

For quick cleanings, liberally sprinkle baking soda over carpet and let it sit for at least 15 minutes before vacuuming. On a monthly basis, sprinkle the baking soda on before going to bed, rub it into the carpet with a broom or brush, and vacuum it up in the morning.

Clean carpet stains

Mix together equal parts baking soda and salt. Brush it gently over the stain and let it sit for a few hours. Vacuum up. Alternatively, make a paste of baking soda and water, rub it into the stain, let it dry, then vacuum up or brush away.

Freshen the wastebaskets

Pour some baking soda in the bottom of a new liner and also sprinkle some in as you add trash to the container, especially smelly stuff like tuna cans and milk cartons. Periodically wash the container with a solution of baking soda and water (1 cup per gallon of water).

Make an inexpensive plaster

Add just enough white glue to baking soda to make a paste. Apply to cracks with finger. (Intended as a temporary solution.)

Remove rust from nuts and bolts

Cover them first with baking soda, then pour vinegar over them and allow to set until bubbling action stops. Scrub with a brush and wipe dry.

Remove water spots from wood floors

Rub with baking soda on a damp rag or sponge. Don't let the wood get really wet, and make sure to dry well.

Deodorize a smoke-filled room

Fill a plant mister with a solution of 4 tablespoons baking soda and 1 quart of warm water. Spray into smoky air to cut the haze and odor.

Freshen ashtrays

Sprinkle baking soda in the bottom of ashtrays to minimize stale tobacco odors. When you empty the ashtray, add new soda. (Will also help extinguish cigarettes and cigars.)

Clean silk plants

Clean silk (and real) plants by washing them in a solution of 1/2 cup baking soda and 1 gallon of cold water. A safe way to make indoor greenery greener.

Restore a rosary

Soak in a baking soda and water solution for ten minutes. Brush gently and rinse clean. Will help restore the tarnished silver and clouded crystal beads of old rosaries.

Make a jewelry cleaner

Make a paste out of baking soda and dish soap (or shampoo). Apply it to jewelry with a toothbrush, rub gently to get in all the little nooks and crannies. Rinse clean and dry with a soft cloth.

PETS AND PESTS

Dry clean the dog

When there's no time for a bath, rub baking soda into dog's fur, then comb it out. Cleans and deodorizes.

Soften the dog's bath water

Add 2 tablespoons of baking soda to your dog's bath water and to the rinse water. His coat will come out clean, soft, and shiny.

Freshen the dog's breath

Brush dog's teeth with a toothbrush dipped in a baking soda solution.

Deodorize pet bedding

Sprinkle baking soda over surface (only if dry). Let sit for 15 to 30 minutes, then vacuum or shake out. For stronger odors, leave the baking soda on longer.

Clean up accidents

Clean as thoroughly as possible and allow to dry. Then sprinkle baking soda on the affected spot to fight lingering odors. Allow to dry, then vacuum or brush off.

Wash the dog collar

Using a brush, scrub the collar with a solution of baking soda dissolved in hot water to remove grease and grime. Nylon collars can be soaked in a solution of equal parts baking soda and vinegar in hot water for 15 to 30 minutes. Rinse and hang up to dry.

Clean pet's toys and dishes

Soak everything in a solution of 4 tablespoons of baking soda and 1 quart of warm water. Scour with dry baking soda if necessary.

Freshen the kitty litter

Spread a layer of baking soda on the bottom of the pan. Then cover with litter.

Deodorize small animal cages

Control odors in hamster, guinea pig, rabbit, and bird cages by sprinkling baking soda on the bottom of the cage and then covering with normal bedding (wood shavings, corn cob, newspaper, etc.).

Clean small animal and bird cages

Wipe all surfaces with baking soda sprinkled on a damp sponge. Rinse and dry. Clean and deodorize aquarium-type cages by putting the aquarium in the sink (or shower or tub if too big), filling it with water and 1/2 cup of baking soda. Let it sit for a while and then easily scrub it clean.

Adjust the pH level in aquariums

High acid levels in aquariums can be dangerous to your fish. Lower them by adding 1/4 teaspoon of baking soda per 10 gallons of water. Continue to test the pH level on a regular basis to keep the level consistent.

Wash horses' legs

Clean the dirt and grime from horses' legs by washing them with a solution of baking soda and water.

Get rid of skunk smell

Bathe your dog in a tub of water which has in it one box of baking soda, the juice of 2 lemons, and a squirt of shampoo.

Remove porcupine quills

Mix two teaspoons of baking soda in one cup of vinegar. Apply to quill area and wait 10 minutes. Reapply and wait another 10 minutes. Quills should then come out easily.

Get rid of ear mites

With a solution of warm water and baking soda, wash the insides of your animal's ears to eliminate itching and ear mites.

Keep pests out of the food dishes

Sprinkle baking soda around outside food dishes. This usually deters insects from approaching and is safe for your pet.

Keep pests out of your home

Prevent carpenter ants, roaches, and silverfish from invading by laying down a barrier of baking soda under sink-pipe openings, along basement windows, and other likely entry points. When it is eaten by insects, the soda creates carbon dioxide bubbles that kill them.

Kill pests in your home

Place a mixture of equal parts baking soda and sugar in infested area. Bugs are attracted to the sugar and will consequently eat too much baking soda.

GARAGE AND SHOP

Deodorize the car

Sprinkle baking soda over carpeted areas, cloth upholstery, and in the trunk. Let sit for as long as possible (overnight ideally) before vacuuming.

Clean vinyl seats

Wipe down with either a baking soda solution or baking soda sprinkled on a damp sponge. Will remove harmful grease and oils. For tough stains, scrub with a paste of 3 parts baking soda, 1 part water, and a few drops of dishwashing soap. Rinse with clean water and wipe dry.

Freshen the floor mats

Clean with a baking soda solution. For tough stains, sprinkle on dry and scrub with a brush. Rinse well.

Extinguish cigarette odor

Sprinkle baking soda in the ashtray.

Make a car washing solution

Mix 1/4 cup of baking soda and 1/2 cup liquid detergent in a gallon of water. Use one cup of this solution per pail of warm water.

Fix a bad battery connection

Make a paste of 3 parts baking soda to 1 part water and brush onto corroded battery posts and cable connectors. Rinse and dry. Lightly coat with petroleum jelly to keep terminals trouble-free.

Be prepared for fires

Keep a large container of baking soda in your car, boat, and garage for extinguishing small oil, gas, and engine fires. Stand at a safe distance and toss the baking soda at the base of the flames.

Remove sticky stuff (but not paint) from your car

Safely remove bugs, tar, tree sap, and bird poo off your car by rubbing on a baking soda paste with a damp cloth. Let the paste set for 5 minute before wiping off the goo. Rinse clean and dry with a soft cloth.

Clean your windshields

Remove stuck-on road splatters from windshields by scrubbing with baking soda on a damp sponge. Make sure to clean dirty wipers this way, too, so you don't undo all your hard work with one swipe.

Brighten your headlights

Scour dirt, salt, and bugs off your lights with baking soda on a damp sponge. (Use on chrome trim, bumpers, and hubcaps too.)

Remove gas smell from hands

Deodorize your hands after pumping gas by sprinkling baking soda on them and wiping them clean with a wet paper towel.

Clean oil spots off the garage floor

Wet area and scour with baking soda and a scrub brush.

Unstiffen hardened paint brushes

Boil them in a solution of 1/2 gallon water, 1 cup baking soda, and 1/4 cup vinegar.

Treat an acid spill

Immediately apply baking soda to the part of the body that's come into contact with the acid. Rinse with cold water and repeat treatment.

Neutralize the results of car sickness

If someone has vomited in your car, first clean up what you can, then pour baking soda over the affected area to eliminate the odor, neutralize the acid, and absorb any remaining moisture. After it dries, vacuum up the baking soda and then shampoo the area.

YARD AND GARDEN

Bolster beautiful blooms

Flowers that thrive in alkaline soil (such as geraniums, hydrangeas, and begonias) will produce brilliant blooms when occasionally watered with a weak baking soda solution.

Sweeten tomatoes

Sprinkle baking soda lightly on the soil around tomato plants. Not only will it sweeten the tomatoes by lowering their acidity, but it will also discourage pests.

Make a "green" pesticide

Combine 1 teaspoon baking soda with 1/3 cup cooking oil. Fill a plant sprayer with 2 teaspoons of this mixture and 1 cup of water. Will kill aphids, spider mites, and white flies, but will not harm beneficial insects.

Make a non-toxic fungicide

Mix together 1 tablespoon of baking soda and 1 tablespoon of dormant oil or vegetable oil. Add 1 gallon of water and stir well. Then add 1/2 tablespoon of liquid dish washing soap and stir again. Pour into a plant sprayer and apply as soon as symptoms of fungal diseases such as powdery mildew and black spot appear. Reapply every seven to 10 days. (Best to spray in the early morning or late afternoon.)

Control outdoor ants

Control the ant population by first sprinkling baking soda on their dirt mounds when damp. Wait about 30 minutes and then pour a small amount of vinegar on the ant hill. Ants will ingest the baking soda-vinegar combination with deadly consequences.

Thwart unwanted grass and weeds

Prevent unwanted grass and weeds from growing in sidewalk, driveway, and patio cracks by pouring or sweeping baking soda into the cracks. The soda will stop new weeds from growing and will kill small ones already present.

Kill crabgrass

Wet down the patch of crabgrass, then cover it with baking soda. The crabgrass will start dying in a couple of days. Be careful not to get too much of the baking soda on your good grass!

Keep caterpillars out of the cabbage

And the broccoli and kale too. To kill the small green cabbage worms that love to chomp on your Brassica plants, make a mixture of equal parts baking soda and flour and dust your plants with it. The worms will eat the mix and die within a day or two from it. Reapply as needed.

Add to the compost pile

Pour baking soda directly out of the box onto the compost pile to control odors. It also keeps acidity levels down.

Remove garden grime from hands

Rub baking soda on wet hands and rinse.

Lengthen the lifespan of cut flowers

Dip cut flowers in a solution of baking soda and water to extend their life.

Rejuvenate the greenery

Mix together 1 teaspoon of baking soda, 1/2 teaspoon of clear ammonia, and 1 teaspoon of Epsom salt in a gallon of water. Use about a quart of the solution on each rosebush-size shrub that's lost its luster.

Control outdoor grill flames

Mix a solution of 1 teaspoon of baking soda and 1 pint of water in a plastic spray bottle. When the fire gets too high, spray at the base of the flames.

Clean the grill

Sprinkle baking soda on a stiff, damp brush and scrub where needed. Rinse clean. For tough jobs, use a wire brush and scrub with a baking soda paste (3 parts baking soda to 1 part water). Rinse thoroughly.

Clean the bird bath

Sprinkle the bird bath with baking soda and scrub away scum with a brush. Rinse well and refill with fresh water. Nothing toxic will be left behind to harm your feathered friends.

Clean the patio furniture

Make a solution of 1/2 cup baking soda, 1 tablespoon dishwashing liquid, and 1 gallon of hot water. Wash, rinse, and dry. (Can also be used to clean the plastic mesh umbrella, but check for colorfastness first.)

Make icy steps less slippery

Shake baking soda on icy steps and porches to keep from slipping. Plus, it won't hurt your floor if tracked inside.

SPORTS AND RECREATION

Freshen RV water tanks

Dissolve a cup of baking soda in a gallon of water and use this to periodically flush out your RV's water tanks. Safe for all types of holding tanks. It will eliminate stale odors and help remove mineral build-ups. Drain and flush tanks before refilling. (You don't want baking soda in your drinking water.)

Deodorize the RV

Dispel odors in your RV's cramped space by placing open boxes of baking soda in the refrigerator, bathroom, or wherever the air is "fragrantly challenged."

Control campfires

Keep a box of baking soda nearby while cooking in case of flare-ups or wayward sparks. When it's time to put the fire out, toss handfuls of baking soda on the base of the flames to extinguish them.

"Green clean" the fishing gear

Use a baking soda solution to clean rods, lines, buckets, hooks, and other gear. There's no need to worry about polluting lakes and rivers.

Clean golf clubs

Clean your golf clubs without scratching them by using a baking soda paste and a brush. Rinse well and let dry.

Clean sports balls

Make your sports balls (soccer balls, volleyballs, baseballs, bowling balls, bocci balls, golf balls . . . you name it) look like new by cleaning them with a baking soda solution or baking soda sprinkled on a damp sponge. Rinse and dry.

Deodorize coolers

Before storing coolers and ice chests away for the season, sprinkle baking soda in them to keep them smelling fresh. When spring comes around, take a damp sponge and use the soda that's in there to give them a nice cleaning.

Lighten up the backpack

Baking soda on a camping or backpacking trip can be invaluable. Use it as a deodorant, a toothpaste, a hand cleanser, an odor eater for boots, a salve for sunburns, first aid relief for bug bites, a laundry detergent, a dish washer, a pot scrubber, and an extinguisher for campfires. Did we forget something? Probably.

Freshen smelly sleeping bags

Sprinkle baking soda inside the bag, close it up and shake it so the soda is well distributed. Let it sit for a day or two, then shake out the powder.

Clean a swing set

Clean the plastic seats of your child's swing set by washing them down with a baking soda solution and sponge, or with baking soda sprinkled on a damp sponge. For tough jobs, try using a paste of 3 parts baking soda, 1 part water, and a few drops of liquid dishwashing soap.

Clean the pool toys

Yes, they're in the water a lot, but they still get grimy. Freshen them up with a mix of 1/4 cup of baking soda in 1 quart of warm water. Wipe them down with the solution and rinse. Grimy small toys can be soaked for a while first.

Freshen up the gym locker

Keep an open or vented box of baking soda in your locker.

Sweeten the gym bag

Sprinkle baking soda in a gym bag at night. In the morning shake or vacuum out the powder along with the odors.

CRAFTS AND PLAY

Make a bubbling ball bouncer

Fill a clear glass container with water. Add 1/4 cup of vinegar and 3 teaspoons of baking soda. Toss in lightweight objects such as rice, sunflower seeds, uncooked pasta pieces and watch them "bounce" around in the mixture. At first the items will sink, but soon bubbles created by the baking soda and vinegar will lift them to the surface. Once they reach the surface, the bubbles break, making the objects sink again and starting the process all over. Renew the solution as needed with 3 parts vinegar to 1 part baking soda.

Make an erupting volcano

Turn a flower pot upside down in a shallow pan. (Make sure it has a raised edge to catch the "lava.") Put an empty tuna can (also upside down) on top of the flower pot. Place a small paper or plastic cup upside down on the tuna can. Tape the cup to the tuna can very securely. (You don't want things moving during the "eruption.") Then cover the entire structure with aluminum foil to create a volcanic shape. Paint it if you like to make it look more realistic.

Make a hole in the top of the volcano (which is actually the bottom of the paper cup) and add several spoonfuls of baking soda and a dollop of dishwashing soap. In a separate cup, add some red food coloring to 1/2 cup of vinegar. Pour this through the top hole and watch your volcano erupt!

Do a science experiment

Put 1/2 cup of hot vinegar in one container and 1/2 cup of vinegar that has been chilled with ice cubes in another. Drop a teaspoon of baking soda into each container and compare the different reactions.

Make baking soda footprints

Make or buy stencils of holiday-themed footprints. Sprinkle baking soda over them to create white "footprints" on your carpets. Some ideas might include:

* Bunny footprints leading to Easter baskets
* Santa footprints leading from the fireplace
* Turkey feet running around the house at Thanksgiving
* Heart shapes at Valentine's Day

This is a fun way to mark the holidays with your kids. And it all vacuums up easily.

Make a Welcome Home greeting

Make a WELCOME HOME stencil and put it on your entryway carpet or front porch. Sprinkle baking soda over it to create a fresh, powdery greeting for returning loved ones.

Dry wood for crafts

Place wet wood in a plastic bag with baking soda and leave it for a few days. The soda will absorb moisture and also get rid of odors and bugs.

Clean coins

Clean grimy and corroded coins with a paste of baking soda and water. Use your fingers to rub the paste around the coin's surface. Rinse with water and dry with a cloth. [**Important!** *Many coin collectors advise against cleaning very old or valuable coins, as it could diminish their value. If you have a serious coin collection, it's best to leave it in its original condition.*]

Make it snow on your model trains landscape

Sprinkle baking soda on your "countryside" for a fresh, powdery just-snowed look.

Turn your hair white

Top off your costume for plays and parties by brushing baking soda into your hair to whiten it. As an added bonus it will give your hair a little extra shine when you wash it out.

HEALTH AND HYGIENE

Make a mouthwash

Rinse and gargle with 1 teaspoon of baking soda in 1/2 cup of water. Neutralizes odors instead of just covering them up.

Brush your teeth

Put a little baking soda on a wet toothbrush. Brush normally. Will clean your teeth and neutralize bacterial waste. For extra whitening and germ-killing action, brush with a paste of 3 parts baking soda and 1 part hydrogen peroxide.

[**Note:** *Baking soda will clean your teeth, but keep in mind it doesn't contain fluoride, a substance dentists recommend to help prevent cavities, especially in pre-adult teeth.*]

Undermine underarm odors

Sprinkle baking soda under your arms as a natural alternative to sprays and sticks.

Use as a preshave/aftershave splash

One tablespoon of baking soda mixed in a cup of water can minimize razor burns.

Take as an antacid

Dissolve 1/2 teaspoon baking soda in 1/2 glass of water and drink slowly. Wait 2 hours before taking an additional dosage. Do not take more than 7 1/2 teaspoons in 24 hours (3 1/2 teaspoons if you're over 60 years old). Don't take continuously for more than two weeks.

[**CAUTIONS:** *Consult your doctor before using if you suffer from hypertension or are on a salt-restricted diet. Consult your doctor first if you are pregnant. Do not give to children under 5 years old. Do not take on an overly-full stomach. Make sure the baking soda is completely dissolved before ingesting. Follow the guidelines!*]

Make a mineral replacement drink

Replace salts lost from vomiting and diarrhea with this inexpensive elixir: Add 1 teaspoon of table salt, 1 teaspoon of baking soda, and 4 teaspoons of sugar to 1 quart of boiled water. Stir until clear and then add 1 packet of sugar-free Kool-Aid or similar flavored drink powder. Store in the refrigerator. (Best to make a fresh batch daily.)

Soothe minor burns and rashes

Apply a paste of 3 parts baking soda and 1 part water or witch hazel. (Also good for poison ivy itch.)

Treat acid spills on skin

Immediately flush the spot with cool water and then cover with baking soda to neutralize the acid. Repeat treatment as needed.

Treat blisters

While bathing in lukewarm water, apply handfuls of baking soda to blisters from shingles and other rashes so that a paste forms.

Soothe poison ivy and chicken pox rashes

Add 1/2 cup of baking soda to a warm bath and soak for a good long while. Also try applying baking soda directly to the skin and holding it in place with a wet cloth.

Treat a bee sting

Apply a paste of baking soda and water on the sting as quickly as possible. (For a wasp sting, it is better to apply vinegar.) If the stinger is visible, try to scrape it off or flick it away. Don't squeeze it with fingers or a tweezers, as this could inject more venom into the skin.

Soften and remove earwax

Fully dissolve 1/2 teaspoon of baking soda in 1 tablespoon of warm water. Using a sterile eyedropper, put a few drops in the ear once or twice daily for several days. (It may help to lie on your side while doing this.) The wax will eventually work its way out of the ear canal where it can then be removed with a cloth or tissue. [**Note:** *Do not use this on someone with tubes in their ears.*]

Fight athlete's foot

Make a baking soda paste and rub it between your toes. Leave it on for 15 minutes, then rinse and dry your feet thoroughly. Also, dusting your shoes and socks with baking soda before wearing them reduces foot moisture which attracts fungus.

Relieve canker sores

Gently rinse your mouth with a solution of 1 teaspoon of baking soda in 1/2 glass of warm water.

Zap zits and blackheads

Make a thick paste of baking soda and water and apply to problem areas. Leave it on overnight and wash thoroughly in the morning.

Soothe a sore throat

Melt 1 aspirin in 2 teaspoons of hot water. Add 1 teaspoon of baking soda, an additional 1/2 cup of hot water, and stir gently. Gargle to ease sore throat discomfort. Repeat as needed.

Clear a stuffy nose

For adult nasal passages, mix 1/4 teaspoon of baking soda with 1 tablespoon of water. Stir to dissolve. Place a drop or two in each nostril. Shortly afterwards you should feel relief from the stuffiness.

Freshen a cast

Use a hair dryer to blow some baking soda inside a cast to help eliminate odors.

Clean dentures and other oral appliances

Soak dentures, retainers, and mouthpieces in a solution of 2 teaspoons of baking soda dissolved in a small bowl of warm water. Brush loose food particles away and rinse. Alternatively, scrub them with baking soda on a wet toothbrush.

Soften bathwater (and skin)

Add 1/2 cup of baking soda to your bathwater to soften hard water and leave your skin feeling silky smooth. A great alternative if you're allergic to bubble baths.

Soothe itchy skin

Itchiness caused by dry skin or psoriasis can be reduced by applying a weak solution of baking soda (1/3 cup soda to 1 gallon of water) to the affected area with a washcloth.

Treat your feet

Give your tired toes a soak in a solution of 4 tablespoons of baking soda and 1 quart of hot or warm water. Also softens calluses and relieves the itch of athlete's foot.

Take a sponge bath

Fill a sink halfway with warm water and add several tablespoons of baking soda. Use a washcloth or sponge to wash all over for a quick, refreshing clean up.

Take care of "down there"

Sprinkle baking soda over inner thighs and genital areas to absorb moisture and deodorize.

Deodorize sanitary pads

Sprinkle a coating of baking soda over a sanitary pad before using for extra deodorizing protection.

Soften rough elbows

Apply a paste of baking soda and water to smooth away rough skin on elbows.

Clean your nails

Dab some baking soda on a small brush and gently clean the tops of your nails as well as under the exposed part. Rinse thoroughly with water. This is a great way to scrub away garden dirt. Works on toenails too.

Dissolve hairspray buildup

Rub a tablespoon of baking soda into lathered hair when shampooing. Rinse and condition as usual.

Clean your toothbrush

Give your toothbrush a thorough cleaning by soaking it overnight in a baking soda and water solution.

Clean grooming accessories

Soak brushes, combs, curlers, cosmetic sponges, and applicators overnight in the sink in a solution of hot water and 1/4 cup of baking soda.

Relieve nicotine withdrawal

Dissolve 2 teaspoons of baking soda in a glass of water and sip slowly. The effervescent liquid relieves the urge to smoke for some people. (Use occasionally. Not recommended for long-term use or for those suffering from peptic ulcers.)

Reduce sugar cravings

Dissolve about 1 teaspoon of baking soda in a glass of warm water and rinse your mouth out (don't swallow the water). The baking soda sets off a chain reaction in your mouth that makes you secrete saliva and appeases your craving for something sweet.

BIBLIOGRAPHY

Bader, Myles. 2001 Food Secrets Revealed. Las Vegas, Nev: Northstar Pub, 1997.

Berthold-Bond, Annie. Better Basics for the Home: Simple Solutions for Less Toxic Living. New York: Three Rivers Press, 1999.

Ciullo, Peter A. Baking Soda Bonanza. New York: HarperPerennial, 1995.

1801 Home Remedies. NY: Reader's Digest, 2004.

Heloise. Handy Household Hints from Heloise: Hundreds of Great Ideas at Your Fingertips. Emmaus, Pa.: Rodale, 2010.

How to Clean Practically Anything. Yonkers, N.Y: Consumer Reports Special Publications, 2002.

Lansky, Vicki. Baking Soda: Over 500 Fabulous, Fun, and Frugal Uses You've Probably Never Thought of. Deephaven, MN: Book Peddlers, 1995.

Noyes, Amy K. Nontoxic Housecleaning. White River Junction, Vt: Chelsea Green Pub, 2009.

Proulx, Earl. Yankee Magazine's Vinegar, Duct Tape, Milk Jugs & More: 1,001 Ingenious Ways to Use Common Household Items to Repair, Restore, Revive, or Replace Just About Everything in Your Life. Dublin, N.H.: Yankee Books, 1999.

Siegel-Maier, Karyn. The Naturally Clean Home: 150 Super-Easy Herbal Formulas for Green Cleaning. North Adams, MA: Storey Pub, 2008.

Wilen, Joan, and Lydia Wilen. Shoes in the Freezer, Beer in the Flower Bed: And Other Down-Home Tips for House and Garden. New York: Simon and Schuster, 1997.

In addition to the above, a myriad of other resources were consulted to put together this compendium of information, including, but not limited to, online tips forums, blogs, and articles. While too numerous and impractical to list individually, the author would like to acknowledge one resource in particular, the Arm & Hammer website (www.armandhammer.com). In addition to many useful solutions, the site offers visitors information about the company's many products as well as the opportunity to sign up for valuable coupons. Check it out!

ABOUT THE AUTHOR

M.B. Ryther is a freelance writer whose work has appeared in a variety of print and online magazines, including *Country Woman*, *Mother Earth News*, *Woman's World*, *Catholic Digest*, *L.A. Parent*, and *Boys' Life*. She lives in Washington State with her husband and four children.